Lovely
CHUBBLY

Tom Stocks

To Katie (my milF BFF)

Thank you For your support
lovely sitting with you
hope you enjoy X

Love Tom X

(chubby Northerner)

BENT KEY
Publishing

First published in Great Britain by Bent Key Publishing, 2022
Copyright © Tom Stocks, 2022
The moral right of the author has been asserted.

ISBN: 978-1-915320-01-8

Bent Key Publishing
Owley Wood Road, Weaverham
bentkeypublishing.co.uk

Edited by Rebecca Kenny @ Bent Key
Cover art © Samantha Sanderson-Marshall @ Smash Design and Illustration
smashdesigns.co.uk

Printed in the UK by Mixam UK Ltd.

If you are looking for beautiful, eloquent poetry -
This book is probably not for you

CONTENTS

NOT FOR ME

For so long, I thought poetry was not for me -
To be in this world, I thought I needed a literary degree,
Not be a lad who only just scraped a C in English at GCSE.
For so long I felt excluded -
Deluded -
But I decided I would give this a go.
I never thought I would meet other poets and go toe-to-toe
As an outsider looking in, I always thought
This stuff was for the elites -
Not a working-class lad from the Bolton streets.
The fact is - growing up, poetry never interested me
It was all *thou*, *thus* and articulating my Ts -
When really, all I wanted was for class to end
So I could go and do keepy-uppies.
But now? I realise I hadn't found the right voice
Because in school, you're given no other choice.
Shakespeare, Poe, Wilde - those were the ones we had to earmark
When we should also have Barrington, Argh Kid -
John Cooper-Clarke;
We need to make poetry more accessible
So people can be taught to be more... expressible?
You don't need to be a literary buff to understand
(Though wish someone had told me that beforehand)
So let's discover new voices and take out the... pretention
Then - you will see more people pay attention

Lovely
CHUBBLY

LOVELY CHUBBLY BODY POSITIVITY

HERE'S TO THE LADS

Here's to the lads that are worried about their weight
Worried about the thoughts of their next Tinder date.
Here's to the lads who cover their belly when they sit
Folding their arms across 'coz they feel like shit.
Here's to the lads whose shirts pop open when taking a seat
Aware our flab seeps through like a piece of meat.
Here's to the lads who have stretch marks on their tummy
And avoid mirrors 'coz they make 'em feel crummy.
Here's to the lads who have let themselves go a bit -
Got into a relationship and aren't as fit;
Here's to the lads that are scared of the gym
Conscious of being judged by muscle-men or someone slim.
Here's to the lads who constantly sweat
Just because they're a bit heavy-set.
Here's to the lads who do fad diets or skip meals
And are fed up of salads and shit healthy meal deals.
Here's to the lads who, when shopping for clothes,
Find they're either too baggy or too tight
Trying on reams of clothes, 'coz they don't quite fit right -
Here's to the lads who are always the butt of the fat joke
But can't let it get to them, because they're a bloke.
Well, lads - I say fuck 'em
They're shallow and dumb.
So here's to you -
My big-boned, chubby, chunky, plump, voluptuous lads
You are sexy, you are attractive, you are hot -
So let's show the world what we've got.
Beauty, sexiness and self worth
Shouldn't be measured by your size
We shouldn't be fed these constant lies.
Don't conform to what society says,
'Coz you've got sex appeal for bloody days!

ACCESSIBLE FOOD

Why is a bag of chicken nuggets a quid
But a pack of chicken breasts is twice the price to feed your kid?
It's not hard to work out that to be consistently healthy,
You need to be a little bit wealthy.
On average, less-healthy food is £5.21 per 1,000kcal;
It's hard to afford free range, organic or halal.
£7.49 per 1,000kcal is the cost of the fresher alternative,
Which I find depressing, but it's informative -
So to eat healthier its an extra £2.50?
I find that more than a little bit shifty.
We need to teach kids in schools healthy foods to cook,
Not pizzas, flapjacks or pies from a basic recipe book -
It's crazy the amount of people
Who haven't been shown how to make a decent meal,
And would much rather sit with a microwave dinner
Followed by a Wagon Wheel.
We need to make nutritional food more accessible
So we are not pumping our bodies with crazy chemicals -
Because it should never be a choice
Between health or wealth.

DAD BOD OR DEMI-GOD?

OK - let's talk about body positivity for men
Where representation needs to be spoken about, again.
Are we still really in a society that prefers
The body of a god to a bad bod?
Men are comparing themselves to a superhero squad.
In our heads we think we need to be something from Marvel. DC.
Well, stop comparing - that's the key.
That puts on the pressure to work towards an unrealistic body.
Also - the rise of social media doesn't help the situation,
Where 43% of us upload gym selfies across the nation.
I'm so over TV shows, films and the 'gram -
It's hard to escape the image of a muscular man.
It's easy for guys to beat themselves up because
They feel they don't fit the norm,
Are constantly pressured to conform -
Because it's the connotations that go alongside it;
You can't be brave, honourable and masculine if you're not fit.
Everyone is different, so there is no need to dwell
It doesn't matter if you're small, medium, large or XL,
But if you only put one type of body in the media -
Marketing. Modelling.
To men, this can be quite telling -
We need to do more on representing.
Firstly - embrace your body, no matter your size
It doesn't matter if you have a belly or thick thighs.
Secondly - talk about this. Normalise it in everyday life,
Whether it be with friends, family or even your wife;
Thirdly - don't be afraid of feeling vulnerable
Even if it makes you feel uncomfortable.
Finally - don't compare yourself to someone unrealistic,
Because it will just lead to you exploding, ballistic.
If you're happy and healthy, who cares what people say?
Don't let the haters ruin your day.

MAN UP

Stop putting men down with phrases of toxicity,
Questioning their male authenticity -
Oh, just Man Up.
Every man, boy or lad has heard this term
Probably from another male trying to stand firm.
Don't be a wimp. Man Up, mate -
Using it as if he's trying to motivate.
I try to hold my breath and not take the bait
But I can't; I fucking hate that phrase -
It makes me descend into a kind of red haze.
It's an out-of-date term used to put men down
Usually said by some cocky, dick-swinging clown.
Or if it's not *Man Up*, it's *take it like a man*,
Once again insinuating I'm below, or less-than.
Or *give over, boys don't cry*,
God forbid tears come from my own eyes -
I forgot, I'm supposed to bottle it up, push it down and lie.
And because I'm a bit chubby, it doesn't give you clearance
To take the piss out of my appearance.
Underweight. Overweight. Lack of definition -
None of these insecurities give you permission.
And if I tell you to stop, you'll say I'm a soft wanker
But we need to listen. Talk. Not pass it as banter.
This is a really tough time for men -
These phrases contribute to male suicide rates rising again.
They're at the highest peak in over a decade -
Don't believe me? Look online. It's all clearly displayed.
Now, I'm not saying these terms are solely responsible,
'Coz they're not.
But we need to accept, recognise, realise and not fantasise
That mental health doesn't exist
Or it could end in another statistic or opportunity missed.

I admit - it's not so much about the singular word or phrase
But the context in which they are being used -
It can leave your mind and self-worth feeling bruised.
We need to pick each other up; create a safe space
Open to discuss any problem we want to face -
Just ask if he's alright over a coffee, pint or ale.
Don't suffer alone just because you're male.
If you have a problem, no matter how small
Grab the phone and give your mate a call.
Think before making that comment on his weight -
Those passing comments can often suffocate.
Break the stigma, take a stand
Accept if he's reaching out a hand -
Let's redefine being a 'macho man'
And come up with a different plan.
Let's get rid of this stiff-upper-lip mentality
Break this outdated abnormality -
Let's make it a formality that men stand in solidarity.
Instead of using words of violence,
Why not check in. See if your mates are suffering in silence.

THE F WORD

You fat fuck. You fat pig. You fat waste of space;
The venom now put behind the term *fat* is a disgrace.
How has a medical term for layers of flesh become an insult?
My tolerance has deteriorated as I have grown into an adult.
Fat Fighters. Fat Camp -
Our bodies publicly weighed and scrutinised for a gold stamp?
I don't mean to preach or be excessive;
I just feel the term *fat* has become aggressive.
Little word-based changes can be so progressive,
And in turn, less hurtful. Less depressing.
So let me share, advise and educate
On things not to say about people's weight:
Pot bellied, round, stout, heavy, solid, podgy;
Flabby, paunchy, dumpy, meaty, beefy, tubby, porky -
(I'm also well aware that sounds like
The chubby remake of The Seven Dwarves.)
And when I walk in to watch the football,
Don't say *hey, big man*, 'coz I'm not that tall -
I know what you're referring to -
But I'll just stay silent, take it on the chin
And say *two pints, thank you -*
So hear out my epiphany; revel in this serendipity
And together, come away from this toxicity.
Instead of calling me a *flab sandwich,*
Think again about your language -
Because it's banter like that which can be misplaced,
And I'm fed up of being the one left red-faced.
I won't keep quiet for any longer;
Calling people out will only make us stronger.
So let's start building better foundations
By acknowledging destructive words and their connotations.
This is the start of my campaign to be heard,
And I'll start by getting rid of the 'F' word.

WEIGHT COMMENTS

Whether you think they look bad or great,
Let's stop commenting on people's weight.
Instead of worrying if your comment might be derogative,
Just appreciate someone is body positive.

WEIGHT CAPABILITY

Don't let your weight define you.

How much did Shakespeare weigh
When writing a soliloquy?
How much did Einstein weigh
When developing the theory of relativity?

Who cares about the weight of Poe, Darwin or Da Vinci?

Your weight doesn't define your capability.

CHUBBY LOVE

Being chubby is not all it's cracked up to be -
Because as time goes by, you often end up feeling ugly.
I used to hate catching glimpses as I got undressed,
Staring at my stretch marks, disgusted. Unimpressed.
Stroking the swollen rolls under my chin,
Wishing it could be sucked out or popped with a pin.
Forcing flat the moobs on my chest (which is beginning to sag) -
Struggling to even see my own dick because of the flab
Fretting at who would wanna give me a shag.
How can anyone ever want me
When I don't even like my own body?
Over-analysing and hating what I see,
It's a constant battle with low self-esteem.
So I hide away from my naked reflection,
Trying not to give my body any further inspection.
Through welled-up eyes,
We use layers as a disguise
As we wish we were a smaller size -
Struggling with our bodies in our toughest times -
We still put a smile on and act like it's fine.
But don't let that fake smile fool you,
Because it's just a suppression, a make-do.
Insecurities take a hell of a long time to accept,
To friends and family, these anxieties are well-kept.
I know it sounds cliché,
But there are people battling this every day.
I'm here to tell you, you don't need anyone's validation -
You're in control of your own narration;
But to overcome any battle with health,
You need to first work on yourself.

LOVELY CHUBBLY RANTS

A RIGGED SYSTEM

I just want to set the record straight -
We don't want things handed to us on a plate.
What we want is for the playing field to be fair;
We don't just want free healthcare -
We want you to stop selling it off
And for our taxes to be equally shared.
We don't want money for doing nowt,
Or a free government handout -
We just want our wages to cover our basic costs,
And stop feeling that somewhere, we've been double-crossed.
We don't want the rich to pay everything for us,
We just want them to pay their fair share, like everyone else does.
A free place to live was never our intent -
We're just asking for affordable housing and rent.
We want our votes and our voices to be heard.
I don't understand why this comes across as so absurd -
So I will shout it - loud and proud
Until the system isn't rigged towards a certain crowd.

GENERATION RENT

First published in Buzzin' Bards, 2022

So - I'm part of this *Generation Rent*,
Where it's near impossible to save that deposit of five percent.
We live in these sub-par accommodations,
Paying sky-high rent just because of the OK location.
Ignore the broken taps, draughts and bad heat circulation
'Coz you have the good transport links of a nearby train station.
It's a catch twenty-two -
We are forced to believe we should just be grateful to have
A roof over our head,
Or you're threatened with
Well, there's always somewhere else instead.
So we live in fear of a landlord,
Terrified of damaging things like a skirting board,
Because your entire existence strives towards
Getting that deposit back.
It turns into a game show, avoiding any broken setbacks,
But we all know it's a fixed competition -
No matter how you leave the housing, the condition,
When renting you never, ever settle
And are always looking over your shoulder,
Wishing they'd sort out the ever-growing black mould and
They can kick you out with no explanation at the drop of a hat,
Hand you a Section 21 - just like *that*.
You live by their rules and they make sure you don't forget -
No kids, no smoking, no decorating - not even a pet
And if they find out you have disobeyed,
Your 2 months' notice comes through straight away.
Then, you start the renting game again
Moving through the gears of stress and strain,
Your earnings, background and credit, all under the microscope,
Then come the deposit and admin charges (which are a joke)

It just makes you think - if I just stopped having to do this,
I could probably afford a house for me and my Miss.
You go to the bank who aren't sure if you can afford
A mortgage repayment of £400,
Well, Mr Bank Manager - look at my background.
You can see I've been paying £900 in rent for the past 10 years,
And you have fears I can't repay half of what I'm paying now?
Right. Cheers.

The system needs a big revamp
Because for us, getting on the ladder
Is looking
Pretty damp.

CONSUMPTION

If there were five words on which I wish people would refrain,
It's *I'm never gonna drink again* -
Oh shut up, you bell-end
We all know you're gonna be out again next weekend.
Taking hungover pictures in your uni dormitory
And posting for attention on your Insta stories -
Judging how good your night was based on the alcohol you drank
Comparing who had more, like a couple of planks -
Bragging about it like a badge of honour
While your room stinks of Sourz, shame and lamb doner -
Maybe I'm blinded by my own presumption -
But don't measure fun by alcohol consumption!

CLASS FINES

It always baffles me that breaking the law can end with a fine.
Surely that can only ever affect people on the breadline?
A punishment that only affects the lower class
And not someone of top brass?

WHAT'S THE RUSH?

Why are people in their 20s and 30s under constant pressure?
Our lives always seem up for measure -
Our friends and family have us surrounded
Always making us feel hounded
By talk of children, houses or an engagement;
I'll do them when I'm ready - not for your entertainment.
How can I bring a child into this world when everything I own
Is either rented or on loan?
What if at this time I have no interest in kids? Bibs? Wiping skids?
Because God forbid
I wanna go travelling from China to Madrid
Or put time and effort into my career,
Or simply just admit I'm not ready for responsibility
And wanna just chill with a beer.
That's OK.
Why is it if you get to twenty-five,
And haven't got the kid, dog and four-wheel-drive,
That's seen as a surprise?
Why, when you approach thirty,
Is not being settled down seen as dirty?
Then, when you surpass that age,
And still don't have any of that - it causes outrage?
Apparently as soon as you hit the big 3-0, that's it. You're done;
The countdown has begun.
You're no longer allowed to have fun.
It's time your life became serious -
You've lost sight. Become delirious -
So what is it? What's the rush?
Why does it matter what someone else is doing,
Prioritising or pursuing?
You just come across so overbearing
With your constant, never-ending comparing.

You have no idea what other people have gone through,
So please have some sensitivity around this, too.
We all have our timeline and that's fine.
So if you've got children, a mortgage, a husband or wife
Great, fantastic - but that's *your* life.
Please don't push your ideals or timeline onto mine.
Please don't ask me when I'm getting married, buying a house
Or having kids again -
Just get lost. Shut up.
Stay in your own lane.

INFLUENCER

God, I hate these fitness influencers aged just shy of 21 -
The ones with neon leotards, tattoos or a man-bun.
Most of us were slim and hot at that age,
So their incessant preaching just fills me with rage.
On TikTok & Insta, pretty as a poodle;
Back then, our diets were fags, booze and a Pot Noodle.
Our exercise was walking to parties and dancing all night,
Even the occasional 3am fight.
Your secret is this - you're just choc-full of youth,
Years of beers, full-time jobs and kids hasn't hit you yet,
And that's the honest truth.
So - continue to preach. Stream your workouts in the park,
But come back to me when you're past the 30 mark.

PUNCHIN'

I hate the term *punchin'* -
A snap judgment based on if someone is stunnin'
A comparison between two people walking down the street,
Rating them like they're pieces of meat.
And look - at some point we've all made a snide remark
When we've seen a couple holding hands in the park -
How the fuck did he get her? He must have a big dick -
Or maybe he's just a nice guy - unlike you, ya prick.
Oh, how did she get him? She must give a good blow job -
Or maybe she's really supportive, or a good laugh - so shut ya gob.
But genuinely, though - in what world do we think
Comments like that are acceptable?
Those shallow views are so unethical -
Thoughts and phrases led by jealousy;
We have no idea of that couple's chemistry or history.
So I'm here to tell you it's OK
If you're a bit bigger than your husband or wife,
If people comment, it just means they're sad in their own life.
Who cares if someone's partner is smaller? Taller?
Or is a different ethnicity or physicality?
It shouldn't matter if one has pecs and the other has specs -
None of this affects someone's capability
To connect with a person's personality
And if you think it does, maybe look
To change your own mentality.
As long as you're in love and happy,
Let's ignore the people who make us feel crappy.

SHUT UP AND REMEMBER

It's that time of year - where flu blocks our sinuses,
The temperatures drop to the minuses,
Weather warnings come out in full force,
Out come the big coats (and the pumpkin spice, of course) -
Hallowe'en has been given the all-clear
There's moaning: *Christmas ads get earlier every year*
It's party season in pubs and bars
But a certain event can fall under your radar -
Who cares? It was over 100 years ago, right?
Well, families across the UK don't forget the fight-
The sacrifices their loved ones made
And the horrific price that they all paid.
Fathers and sons stared down the barrel of enemy guns
Wives losing their Mr -
Brothers losing their sisters -
Over 100 million people died in these two wars -
Not forgetting the 457 in the Afghan and Iraq tours.
Your soldiers, sailors, airmen and all;
Those heroes have always answered the call.
Tears filled the nation's eyes,
As they all said their painful goodbyes -
Their loved one's return shadowed in uncertainty...
Those years of war felt like an eternity.
Brave people gave us their blood and sweat
To give you the right to moan on the Internet -
So Lest We Forget
Whatever the colour of your poppies
Remember our earth is composted by fallen bodies
This day shouldn't be used for any agenda or personal gain
It's a day to think about sacrifice and pain
We should reflect and respect
Not object and dissect

Let us be grateful it's not *us* going to war
And appreciate what our ancestors fought for.
Whatever your political belief,
Just be glad it's not your family laying down a wreath -
So, six words of advice
For this November:
Be respectful.
Shut up and remember.

GRAMMAR POLICE

One of my biggest pet hates is the grammar troll,
Getting kicks out of correcting a tweet for the LOLs;
If I send a text in a mad rush,
I don't need you wading in with your grammar brush.
I couldn't care less if its *your* or *you're*,
Their or *there*, *wear* or *where*.
My message to you wasn't meant to be a literary exam -
It was a simple question on where you wanted to get some scran.
Nobody is ever going to say *thank you for correcting me - and so quick!*
It just makes us think -
Get a life, ya prick

THE INVISIBLE MAN

Help out the homeless -
We've been let down by a nation
More interested in war and invasion
Than helping kids sleeping in a railway station.
No home, no money,
Wishing we could phone our mummy
To just once, put a hot meal in our tummy.
Busking and begging for our next bit of coin
While the rich feast on dinners of plump pork loin -
Walking past me, avoiding my gaze
Pretending you're in some sort of daze - a haze - not fazed,
Not caring that I've been out here for days.
I'm just an invisible man; that's all I am -
Living in my home-street-home
No money, just a shit tent to call my own
That I sit in alone, no family to 'phone.
In life I wasn't dealt a fair hand,
My Mum telling me I was unplanned -
Picking a man, over her own son,
Throwing me out like I was nowt.
A high school drop-out.
But I don't want you to feel sorry for me,
No -
I want you to stand up and fight
Because I have a right
To step out of this doorway and into the light
Give me a chance to get back on my feet
Get me off this fucking street, into heat with something to eat;
So at night when you feel the temperature drop -
I'm asking, Britain - remember what you've got

LOVELY CHUBBLY LAUGHS

BINFLUENCERS

Every week on a Tuesday night,
A thought pops up and gives me a fright.
I peep through the curtains, trying to be discreet
To see what colour bin is out in the street.
The panic is about to begin
When I see no neighbour has put out their bin.
In disarray, I log onto the council app
When my neighbour pops out in his flat cap.
He's about to save mankind,
As I hear him drag his bin behind -
I rush out, trying to not look so keen
To see if his bin is black, brown or green.
Then I see other neighbours follow his lead
And I realise this guy is a hero with this deed.
Then I think - there must be a *Binfluencer* on every street
Unknowingly helping, every week on repeat.
We admire them from afar,
As their heroism flies under the radar.
So, this is my thank you to all the Binfluencers out there -
Without you, bin days would be looking very bare.
These people can come in all sizes and shapes,
And they are solid proof that not all heroes wear capes.

SITCOM HISTORY

In the 1940s started the age of sitcom power -
With the likes of *Pinwright's Progress* and *Hancock's Half Hour*;
As we enter the 50s: ITV
And we saw the success of the BBC
They realised Hancock's fame
And made their first sitcom: *The Army Game*;
And so now, we enter the swinging 60s,
Where comedy was spread across all TVs;
It seemed everybody had a sitcom
From *Dad's Army* to *Steptoe and Son* -
Most of these overlap into the 70s,
But joined with the likes of John Cleese
Entering the new comedy scene with ease;
We see one icon in his prime with *Fawlty Towers*,
Another hits his stride in *Open All Hours*.
We also see the birth of *The Last of the Summer Wine*,
The longest-running British sitcom of all time.
Something for the working classes was *On the Buses*
Or if you wanted some working-class heart,
You watched *Til Death Us Do Part*.
Then - we enter the 80s, the golden age of sitcom -
While the country battled with Thatcher, unemployment
And an exploding IRA bomb.
Only Fools-ing around we have Rodney, Grandad and Del
On Peckham markets, trying to buy and sell.
Then for the poshos, we had *Yes Minister*;
An insight into MPs being sinister.
But if instead, you fancied some anarchy -
We had *The Young Ones* on a Saturday,
Or, if you wanted a more international show,
We always had *Allo! Allo!*

And if you were after something a bit madder,
We had the lads of *Blackadder*.
Then, whatever the weather,
There was always *Birds of a Feather*.
Now in the 90s, if a flat smelled rotten -
It was almost certainly the hit show *Bottom*.
Or we could visit Dave, Denise, Jim, Barb and Nan,
For a brew with *The Royle Fam*.
Then from The North,
We go into the realm of *Red Dwarf*.
But if you're not a fan of the Red,
Pop in to see *Father Ted;*
If you're young, a teen,
You'd always love the absurd *Mr Bean* -
And if when you're watchin', you're more of a religious picker
Then you'd pop down to Dibley to meet the vicar.
Peter Kay was hitting the heights
With *Max and Paddy* and *Phoenix Nights*
And your mid-week evening was never drab
With the fashionable ladies of *Ab Fab* -
Now, we enter the modern era
From *Motherland* to *Vera*
Channel 4 have started cracking some winners
With *The Inbetweeners* and *Friday Night Dinner*
Cross over to Ireland for four Irish Pearls -
It's the hilarious *Derry Girls*
There are so many others that deserve a mention,
But these sitcoms are perfect for breaking every-day tension.
Sitcoms have always picked me up from my darkest pit
To make me laugh until my sides almost split;
All your problems just melt away
As you escape and forget - for 20 minutes each day.

DEAR KAREN

Dearest Karens of the Internet:
Surprise, surprise! This will piss you off, I bet -
As you're always looking to be offended,
Calling for people to be apprehended;
Why do you have so much time on your hands?
Always moaning if someone is gay, bi, or trans -
Is it fun for you to constantly put people down,
Awarding yourself the social media crown?
Do you show it off and brag to your kids and hubby?
Look, Graham; I just called Adele chubby!
You seem to always have something to say,
Have you literally got nothing else to do with your day?
Spouting your shit about how *All Lives Matter*
Or body-shaming a celebrity, saying they've got fatter;
Moaning about appearances or what people wear,
Don't show cleavage, ladies; Karen will despair!
Whenever I see a Daily Mail article on my feed,
I know a Karen will have been let off her lead.
She's always there lurking in the comments section,
Primed and ready to give her interjection -
How many Ofcom complaints have you made this week?
Foaming at the mouth, gagging to give your critique?
And by God, don't bring up Meghan Markle;
For we all know Karen's thoughts on that debacle.
Anything not white, middle class or British -
She's there, ready to preach,
Once again, droning on about *freedom of speech*.
All the time and effort you put in just to complain -
I can't decide if you're tenacious or just lacking a brain.
An army of key board warriors hiding behind a screen,
A racist, homophobic, sexist, body-shaming team.

You are the voice nobody asked for -
Thrusting forward on your crusade;
A proud member of the PC brigade,
But do us all a favour, Karen - go get bloody laid.

THE LIFE OF A DOG-WALKER

Ah, the morning dog walk -
Where every owner wants to bloody talk.
Yes, please do tell me more of how little Penelope has got the trots
And her stomach is all in knots,
And how tomorrow she's off to the vets for her updated shots.
I love it when their little tails wag,
But then you realise - shit! I forgot a poo bag!
And they're there, squatting on the street,
As you walk off, trying to kick it away with your feet.
I feel when you're dog walking, you're always on edge,
Fretting over whether it's a dog is on a lead
Or a murderer coming out of that hedge.
In the evening, when it's lashing down with rain,
You look at the clock
And say - does she really need walking around the block?
But I wouldn't change it,
Because it's such a great way to exercise your mental health.
Forget the worries of family, careers and wealth.
Because for that hour you just get away
And it's just you and your dog - ready to play.

PASTIES

Now I don't want you to think I'm nasty,
But there is no better food than a pasty.
If you don't think I'm right - I will put up a fight
And say your palate is a big bag of shite.
You might think my statement is odd,
But understand - this is the food of God.
Pound Bakery, Greggs, Pukka or Ginsters;
Nothing will keep you warmer in the Winter.
They can mark any occasion -
Get them anywhere in the nation.
There's nothing better on your lunch break,
Than shovelling down a cheeky Steak Bake.

B & M

British high streets are dying
But there's one place that never stops supplying -
It's withstood the test of time,
Now with 700 stores, it's hitting its prime.
Founded in Blackpool in 1978:
Most stores open from 8am 'til late
When your supplies are running low
There's only one place to go -
When you're late on your rent again,
It's because you've spent it at B&M!

The place you nip in for a cheap brolly
But you come out with a full trolley;
You pop in for a new door handle
But come away with a scented candle;
You promise you're only going in for an extension cable
But you know you're coming away with a new bird table.
From ketchup to barbed wire
Deckchairs to hair dryers
It's stacked with everything your heart desires -
So don't worry if I'm gone for hours,
I'm probably in the garden section buying flowers.
The Swedes came up with Ikea
But us Brits had a better idea -
Sunshine indoors, it's all under one roof
And my composing this poem is proof
That true happiness does exist -
Because you can get everything on your shopping list.

PINK CUSTARD

Who remembers the food at school?
The processed junk that made you drool.
Just as your tummy rumbled, the bell would start to ring,
Which could only mean one glorious thing -
It's time to sprint to that lunch queue,
Ready to see that à la carte menu.
There she is - in her hair net, dressed in green;
Mrs Parson, the canteen queen.
With the face of a bulldog and the smile of a saint,
You get what you're given - with no complaint.
What could it be on the menu today?
Turkey dinosaurs? Smiley faces?
Or the lumpy SMASH that gets stuck in your braces?
Twizzlers, potato waffles and beans?
Or perhaps a slab of soggy, dehydrated greens?
Nuggets, mini-pizzas and spaghetti hoops?
Always from either the fried or greasy food groups -
Anaemic hot dogs and bright-yellow mustard
Followed by sponge with sprinkles and pink custard.
You pray for a slice of Arctic Roll
And not warm Angel Delight in a bowl.
Or if none of these are your kinda thing...
There is always a watery pot of Pasta King.

LOVELY CHUBBLY MEMORIES

A CHILDHOOD IN BOLTON

Ah, good old Bolton.
Once famous for its factories and cotton mills -
Now known for its Pound Bakeries and take-away grills.
It's my home town and I'm proud of where I'm from;
Remember queuing under-age outside Ikon?
It's a bit rough-and-ready but not short of a friendly face,
And at its centre - the historic market place.
It's one of the largest towns in Europe; apparently that's a plus?
A place where the people say *buz* and not *bus*.
All the drivers ask if you're *alreet*,
And the smell of Carr's Pasties wafts through the street.
A place famous for our picturesque Town Hall and crescent;
Even the Peaky Blinders have filmed here, which is pleasant -
A place put on the map by Fred Dibnah and Peter Kay,
Even Top Gear filmed here t'other day.
Where we have never had any other choice
But to say *GARLIC BREAD* in that famous voice.
Our yearly panto at The Albert Hall -
Always followed by a drug-infested pub crawl.
Paved with chipped cobbles and empty shops,
Filled with closing-down sales, 50% off pots and mops.
Sick-filled gutters after a Friday night,
Flocks of lads roaming, ready to fight.
It's covered in terrace houses in symmetrical rows;
Knocked-over wheelie bins shimmer under the moonlight glow.
Littered to the rafters with hard-working grafters;
Overlooked by Winter Hill and Rivi Meadows
And the fleeting chants of football echoes.
We have exquisite cuisine, like the breakfast bin-lid,
And those corner-shop sweets you bought as a kid
And for your tea, some weird meat casserole -
That's why I'm proud of my Bolton 'shithole'.

KNOCK-A-DOOR RUN

Just think - when you last played out,
You never knew that it was your last time -
I'm sure we all wish we could go back
To when playing-out was in its prime.
Now, I think childhoods are dead - I'm sorry, but it's true.
Dwindling are the days of kids playing in the street,
When you played things like Kerby with your old mate Pete
Or did street Olympics like you were a professional athlete.
Gone are the days of *knocking on* and asking if you're playing out
Not coming home on time and getting a clout -
Now kids are shackled up inside, on their 'phone
Mindlessly scrolling like some sort of clone
Or *tap-tap-tapping* away on Fifa and COD;
Getting sucked into a virtual world full of upgrades and mods.
What happened to putting jumpers down? Having a kick about?
Instead they're taking selfies with a trout pout -
Uploading and begging for a comment or like
Instead of crushing a can up
To make your wheel sound like a motorbike
I remember kids having imagination and fun
When you would go to your neighbours' with *Knock-a-Door Run*
Or you'd have water fights, play wrestling, build forts
Smashing British Bulldog and other street sports.
I miss the days of games like *Man Hunt*,
When you'd come home with grass stains all down your front
Where are the little rivalries with your next street along
When you felt invincible and could do no wrong?
Or seeing how fast you could cycle down the hill
Racing against your mates - just for the thrill?
And to finish - there was nothing better
Than coming home from being carefree
And finding turkey dinosaurs on a plate for your tea.

Look at us now, eh?
All across the UK, kids to scared to go out and play -
Now they're smothered and bubble-wrapped inside
Parents too scared to let them out in case they might die.
Without that trust, our streets look bare
No community left there - and that's not fair.
I loved the mates I made on my Bolton cul-de-sac
The ones you knew always had your back,
Because those days taught us a lot growing up.
It teaches you to socialise, to create a friend
Where you can be anything in a world of pretend
Now kids don't even interact face-to-face -
It's a world I just can't comprehend or embrace.
Rather than staying inside with all your worries and doubt...
Go. Knock on a neighbour's door and ask if they're playing out.

NOSTALGIA

Recently I've started to reminisce
Back to the times when our childhoods were bliss.
Our only responsibility
Was feeding our Tamagotchi -
Sitting on seats in parks drinking Lambrini
And our parents' hatred towards our Furby.
Playing with Action Man and Barbie
As we were getting down to an *S Club Party*
While drinking WKD and Bacardi.
We had the choice of either CBBC or CITV;
Keenan and Kel or *Saved by The Bell*
Goosebumps and *Stig of the Dump*
Tracey Beaker and *Blue Peter*
Wallace and Gromit - off to the moon
While we're all Space Jamming to *Looney Toons*.
Tony Hawk teaching us how to skate
While Cilla pairs us up on *Blind Date*.
Kids were watching *Thomas the Tank*
While the adults played *Blankety-Blank*.
Harry catching his first snitch
To *Sabrina the Teenage Witch* -
Total-90 trainers
To arguing who's the best Power Ranger -
Going on adventures with *Biff, Chip and Kipper*
Crying at *Free Willy* waving his flipper
Buying a Panda Pop from the tuck shop.
Oasis and Blur going toe-to-toe,
Swapping cards from *Pokémon* and *Yugi-Oh*
Battling our *Beyblades*
And watching *Johnny Bravo* in his shades
Eminem spitting out exquisite words
5-4-3-2-1 *Thunderbirds!*

Burning CDs for our Walkmen
And playing Snake on our indestructible 3310
Before asking for a cam-to-cam on MSN.
Trying to watch *2 Girls 1 Cup*
While waiting for the Internet to dial up-
Decorating our MySpace and Bebo
And Polaroid was the only way to take a photo
Saturdays were filled with Dick and Dom going bonkers
Then we played *Kerby*, *Man Hunt* and conkers.
Getting high off of scented gel pens
While watching Ross and Rachel unfold in *Friends* -
Playing our Sega Mega Drive
Keepin' on Movin' with 5ive
My Name is Earl
And *Mysterious Girl*
All Rise for Blue
Paul and Barry saying *to me, to you* -
Becks making Posh his wife
Just to Spice-Girl up his life.
At Christmas I prayed for a Buzz or Woody
While Big Brother introduced us to Jade Goody.
In '96 we thought it was coming home
Then a few years later, we opened the Millennium Dome
I hope you've enjoyed my trip down Memory Lane
But watch out!
I still believe that one day
The world will be taken over by *Pinky and the Brain*

TWO WORLDS COLLIDE

Growing up I had two separate passions: theatre and sport.
Because of this, my football and rugby careers were cut short.
Apparently, the two worlds could never collide,
Because I was always forced to pick a side.
Pushed to choose between rehearsal or training
And over time it just got so draining -
One came out the winner in the end;
My path took me down into the world of pretend.
But why? Why was it one or the other?
Why could they not exist alongside one another?
Apparently doing both is *breaking the status quo* -
You either play the game or go and watch a show;
Art and sport clashing and going toe-to-toe.
Nah, you can't sing and dance; that's gay -
You can't have a kick around *and* be in a play;
Well - I can, because both things follow the same DNA.
Actually, on closer inspection
The two things follow the same direction!
In both worlds, we visit different-sized venues,
Follow our favourite teams, or celebrities on the news.
You arrive with every intention of being entertained,
Sat shoulder-to-shoulder in seats, often feeling constrained.
Both give us high and lows, following different plots;
Anticipating the next twist, our stomachs in knots.
Each actor or player reviewed after every performance;
Both teams led by a manager, director or someone of importance.
To get to the top, it takes hard work and dedication,
And both engross communities right across the nation.
There are stewards or ushers showing you to your seat,
And specially-designed footwear to put on your feet.
Always overpriced tickets to attend,
To have fun watching with family or friends.

Half-time programmes, drinks and snacks,
Merchandise, branded shirts, caps and backpacks
Equal sets of passionate fans,
Venue and stadium bans,
Costumes, uniforms and kits
Prima donnas, drama queens and massive hissy fits -
Angry guards and season cards,
Singing and chanting,
Panting and ranting...
The list goes on!

So don't ever again ask me to pick a side
Because I love them both - with just the same amount of pride.

FRESH START

Starting fresh is always a scary thing
We all know the kind of stress it can bring.
Leaving your old life behind, walking into a new one feeling blind.
Abandoning friends, jobs, a steady life you've built;
Developing an ever-growing spot of guilt.
Have I made the right choice?
In your head, there is always that voice.
What if this is the wrong decision?
What if it's not what I envisioned?
But you realise that worrying about your next opportunity
Immediately fades when you're welcomed to a new community.
You swap the cramped flat infested with mice
For a suburban house at half the price.
You trade in the huge metropolis and diverse cosmopolis
For the old Northern mills and the long, rolling hills.
Exchange the hot, sweaty underground
For the freezing buses that buzz around.
You switch from the muggy smog that turns your bogies black
To never leaving your house without your *Pac-a-Mac*.
And you know what? It's the best decision I've made,
And it makes you think - *why was I ever afraid?*
I'm home, I'm back where I belong,
Here to stay until my final swansong.
I never regret choosing to leave
Because I'm proud of what I learned and what I achieved.
I had an incredible ride and met amazing people along the way
And all that has led to this new segue.
I left a boy, returned a man
Back to where I began, armed with a new life plan.
Us Northerners are like boomerangs -
We always return with a massive **bang**.
So after my short-lived goodbye
I'm back for a good brew, a pint and a meat-and-potato pie.

PRE-MATCH BUILD-UP

The buzz of the build-up on the bus and trams,
The banter and chants between the travelling fans.
The butterflies as you see the stadium in the distance -
Today, football is your **entire** existence.
Away fans have travelled for miles;
The excitement as you push through the turnstiles
Standing at the top of the stand, overlooking the pitch
Down the steps, seeing every blade of grass and feeling that itch.
Greeting the community you see every week,
Folding down your seat, ready to sit cheek-to-cheek
The smell of Balti pies drifting through the air
As the Baltic wind whistles through your hair.
Dad handing me a Bovril to warm my palms,
Preparing for battle with our brothers-in-arms.
Pre-match music bounces off the walls,
As both teams are out, warming up with the balls.
Emotions and nerves, both unstable;
Checking where a win will put you in the table.
Debating tactics and what the score could be;
Seeing stragglers nip for a last-minute wee,
But, a tip - never go for a poo on match day.
The toilets always look like Guantanamo bay,
No roll and thinking *it's al'reet -*
I'll wipe it with an Aldi receipt.
Pride-filled eyes as they walk onto the grass,
Thinking every player is world-class
And fighting back tears as chants ring in your ears.
There is no better feeling then that pre-match spell,
Anticipation. By the end - will you see Heaven or Hell?
As the players take their positions for war,
The entire stadium erupts in a roar.
Then all eyes on the ref as players take the knee,
I close my eyes and wait for kick-off in *1, 2, 3.*

UP 'ERE

Only up North can you go to a chippy and order Chinese
Then on a school night, go and smash ten pints with ease.
Up 'ere, dinner is called tea and tea is called dinner
And we have bread with everythin'
(That doesn't make us thinner.)
Up 'ere, a Greggs is every half a mile
Because pies and pasties are ingrained in our lifestyle.
Around these parts, it's a barm, not a roll,
We dip 'em in gravy to warm our soul.
Up ere, we all argue on who's got the best family recipes,
Whether its tatty 'ash, hotpot or parched peas.
Up 'ere, we're known to be working class,
Known for our cotton, steel and gas
We were the home of the Industrial Revolution
The world looked to us for our textile solutions.
Up 'ere, we live for the 3pm kick off, a pint and a brawl,
Because that's what you get in the home of football -
You're either a red or a blue - that's the choice
We're the home to Vimto, Kellogg's and Rolls Royce.
Up 'ere, every other pub has karaoke and people looking daft,
Belting out Oasis after a hard day of graft.
Up 'ere, if we call ya *duck* or *cock*,
It's a sign of affection - not an insult to mock.
Around here we say things like *mint, buzzin', angin', swear down*
Where we all refer to Manchester as *town*.
Every winter we flock to the Blackpool Illuminations
And we all get chips on the way back to the station.
We are the home to some of the nation's best-loved shows,
From *Phoenix Nights* to *Corrie's* high and lows.
Up 'ere, we have so many icons. From the Gallagher brothers
To McKellen, Lennon, McCartney and many others.

We're even pioneers for gay and women's rights,
Because we're never afraid to stand up and fight -
That's why we have Rashford feeding our kids
While the government feast on their canteen ribs.
You see, if you're not from up 'ere,
Everyone thinks it's all puddles and struggles,
Or plenty of cobbles but no morals -
But it's the opposite.
Everyone says we're the friendliest people you'll meet,
We welcome anyone in for a brew off the street.
Our hearts are on our sleeve, we're brash and we're proud -
And after a few bevvies, yeah - we can get a bit loud...
But that's who we are.

So raise a glass, whether it's wine or beers,
And all say *we love the North - cheers!*

ACKNOWLEDGEMENTS

With many thanks:

To Jordan-Emma Canavan, Andrew Stocks, Barbara Stocks, and Catherine Stocks - without their constant support I would be nowhere.

To my incredible friends and family.

To Carla Mellor, Stephanie Perry and Matt Concannon - my poetry influencers. To Rebecca Kenny and Bent Key for giving me this wonderful opportunity. To David Scott, BBC Upload and the BBC Radio Manchester team. To the staff over at Spinners Mill and The Royal Exchange Theatre.

To Dad and Cath, for putting up with endless tears, stress, tantrums and for all the curry bribes during GCSEs. To Grandma, who can take a lot of the credit for my writing - for proofreading essays and helping me to understand grammar and structure. If it weren't for you, I would never have overcome that barrier and fear of writing.

To all the venues in Wigan, Leigh and Manchester who have given me my first gigs. To all the incredible poets and wordsmiths who I have been honoured to share the stage with on the Greater Manchester circuit and who have been more than supportive of me.

However, my biggest thanks probably goes to Rhymezone.com, without which I probably wouldn't be a poet.

And, of course, to Bella the dog.

ABOUT THE AUTHOR

It was always drilled into Tom at an early age that he wasn't very academic - he was told by his teachers that he wouldn't receive any GCSEs. A change of schools forced him to knuckle down, and Tom crawled through with 7 Cs and an A across the board.

Shakespeare and Dickens didn't really ignite any passion in Tom. He didn't discover alternative voices until much later in life; he wishes he had discovered these sooner as these voices are the ones that now influence and inspire Tom's poetry and writing.

His debut play *Netflix and Chill* was nominated for a Standing Ovation Award from London Pub Theatres and his most recent play *On the Streets of Covid* won The Royal Exchange's Local Tale Award. He has been featured on several BBC platforms and became the unofficial face of B&M Bargains' Christmas campaign with his viral poem *B&M* in December 2021.

Tom also co-runs his own poetry event in Leigh called The Mic At The Mill at the Leigh Spinners Mill.

ABOUT BENT KEY

It started with a key.

Bent Key is named after the bent front-door key that Rebecca Kenny found in her pocket after arriving home from hospital following her car crash. It is a symbol - of change, new starts, risk and taking a chance on the unknown.

Bent Key is a micropublisher with ethics. We do not charge for submissions, we do not charge to publish and we make space for writers who may struggle to access traditional publishing houses, specifically writers who are neuro-diverse or otherwise marginalised. We never ask anyone to write for free, and we like to champion authentic voices.

All of our beautiful covers are designed by our graphic designer Sam at SMASH Illustration, a graphic design company based in Southport, Merseyside.

Find us online:
bentkeypublishing.co.uk

Instagram/Facebook   @bentkeypublishing
Twitter   @bentkeypublish

WE ARE VIABLE

I'm fed up of entertainment not being seen as a viable career
When someone asks you about your job, it strikes you with fear
Why am I embarrassed about telling them I'm in the arts?
Just wanting to nip the convo in the bud before it starts
You just know the response you're going to get
But why am I worried about the opinion of taxi driver Brett?
Because we have been conditioned that the arts aren't viable?
Told it's just a hobby, a dream, low skilled, not hireable?
Society turns its nose up, saying *get a proper job* -
But I'm fed up of trying to justify myself to snobs.
So I'm here to tell you this industry contributes 900 million
Every single month - that adds up to 10.8 *billion*,
So over the years, we have gifted the economy over a trillion!
(For all you people who can't comprehend it unless it's a stat)
Before you throw your toys out of the pram like a spoiled brat -
Even after all that, here we are again fending for ourselves
While Boris, Cummings, Rishi and Oli think of themselves
As usual, the arts are bottom of the list
Causing us all, yet again, to feel a little pissed
Who's really surprised they've given us the fist?
Understand that our industry is being left to rot
Millions of people now left jobless and in a tight spot
So for all you sceptics out there who say *get a plan B*
Let's see how you get through this pandemic without a TV.
Your Disney, Prime, Netflix subscription - cancel it
Don't go to the cinema to see the next blockbuster hit
Close your books, turn your music off, stop singing that tune
Don't dance to that song that makes you look like a loon
No playing of your favourite video game
Or going on TikTok, trying to claim fame.
Lockdown would have been pretty dire without all of these -
So all I'm asking is this -
Help the arts industry out. Please.